JUMP TO COW HEAVEN

JUMP TO COW HEAVEN

by Gill Adams

WARNER/CHAPPELL PLAYS

LONDON

A Warner Music Group Company

JUMP TO COW HEAVEN
First published in 1998
by Warner/Chappell Plays Ltd
Griffin House, 161 Hammersmith Road, London W6 8BS

ISBN 0 85676 229 6

Printed by Commercial Colour Press, London E7

JUMP TO COW HEAVEN was first performed by Big Fish Theatre Company at the Assembly Rooms, Edinburgh on 8th August, 1997, as part of the Edinburgh Festival Fringe, with the following cast:

JOHN	Martin Freeman
FRANK	Josh Richards
LISA	Sarah Parks

Directed by William Kerley

Designed by Les Stephenson

The production subsequently transferred to the Riverside Studios, London.

JUMP TO COW HEAVEN was awarded the inaugural *First of the Fringe Firsts* Scotsman Award for Best New Play at the 1997 Edinburgh Festival Fringe.

Many thanks to:

Mike Healy and Tom, Neil Rider, Jane Bower, Amanda
Welborn, Jack Bradley, Gill Young, Kevin Hancock, Avril
Could, John Hazlett and Jonathan Baillie. With special thanks
to my daughter Lucy.

AUTHOR'S NOTE

East End of London, Christmas 1966.

The Kray twins decided to spring Frank Mitchell after the
Cornell murder backfired and scared their friends far more
than their enemies. Business was suffering and they needed
something to show the underworld that they were more than
'trigger-happy murderers'. Mitchell, who was known as the
'Mad Axe Man', was to be helped to escape from Dartmoor
then kept in hiding until he could write some letters to the
papers and appeal to have his case looked into. Of course,
most of the credit would go to the twins.

On December 12th, 1966, Frank was driven to a small base-
ment flat in Barking. He was to be given anything he wanted.
John, his minder, was reassured by the Krays that the 'Mad
Axe Man' would be grateful just to be home for Christmas . . .

'They promised Frank everything a man could ever wish for:
freedom, friendship, love, money and a big house in the
country. They sold him a hell of a dream then used it against
him.'

Scene One

The lounge of a basement flat in the East End of London. The flat is small, basic, even tacky in its decoration. A kitchen off stage left, and a bedroom off stage right. JOHN *sleeps on the settee. It should be obvious straight away that* FRANK *is too large for such a confined space.*

FRANK *stands in the middle of the room looking awkward. He's holding a mask and a portable radio. We can see by the look on* FRANK'S *face that he's obviously disappointed, having expected something grander — a hero's welcome from the twins with champagne and girls.*

JOHN   Right mate . . . I'll shove the kettle on . . .

FRANK   Kettle?

JOHN   Yeah . . . I'll fix a brew, bet you're parched, ain't ya?

FRANK   You're gonna make tea?

JOHN   Yeah, and I've got a nice Battenberg saved special . . .

FRANK   What the fuck's that?

JOHN   Eh? Battenberg? Well, it's a cake, it's nice . . .

FRANK   Cake?

JOHN   Yeah. Look, you sit down, make yourself at home . . . I'll see to the tea.

FRANK   Tea and bleedin' cake?

JOHN   Or coffee? Do you prefer coffee?

FRANK   . . . tea and bleedin' coffee . . .

JOHN   So I bet it feels good to be out, eh? Frank?

FRANK   Is this it then?

(JOHN *looks at him, trying to be light.*)

JOHN   Eh? Oh well yeah, I know it's a bit small but we've got everything we need, bathroom's through there, you take the bedroom, nice double bed, electric fire . . . cosy. I sleep out 'ere, settee's knackered but I need to be near the front door. They filled you in on the rest, yeah? Phone and that . . . ?

(FRANK *looks puzzled.*)

JOHN   It rings right, then stops, then rings again, stops, then rings a third time. Then I know it's them. Me right, never you, Frank, just in case. Same with the front door, you never answer it, leave it to me.

FRANK   But Ron said he'd be 'ere.

JOHN   Yeah, but things are a bit tricky right now, so why don't you relax a bit, put your feet up.

FRANK   But Ron said we'd 'ave champagne.

JOHN   Oh well yeah, right, I see, yeah, yeah, well we've got . . . whisky. Yeah? 'Ere mate, you put your feet up and I'll fix you a large one . . .

FRANK   I thought there'd 'ave been a big party or somethin'.

JOHN   Well, I've got cake and I can do you a nice steak an' that . . . you like steak, yeah?

(*He gives him a large whisky.*)

FRANK   Yeah, medium rare . . . Ron said he'd be round an' that. It's gonna be all over the news see, I reckon he wants to listen to it with me.

(FRANK *empties his glass, holds it out for more.* JOHN *fills it reluctantly.*)

JOHN

Yeah, yeah, well maybe tomorrow, eh? Mind you, you're right about the news, it's been on already, I tell you, Frank, they're shittin' themselves. They're calling you "Britain's Most Dangerous Man"! (*Laughs nervously.*) What do they know, eh?

(FRANK *looks at him in thought and then puts his mask on.* JOHN *looks on not knowing what to expect.*)

FRANK

'Ere what do you think of this? (*He groans menacingly.*)

JOHN

Yeah . . . yeah, nice . . .

FRANK

I made it meself out of a woman's nightie. One of the screws brought it in. He thought I was gonna make a washbag.

JOHN

Yeah . . . washbag, eh? Funny.

FRANK

It still smells of her . . . you know, his missus.

(FRANK *lunges forward making* JOHN *jump.* FRANK *laughs.*)

FRANK

What kind of cake is it?

JOHN

Battenberg.

FRANK

Is that the kind of cake you have at parties then?

JOHN

Yeah, that's right. I'll fetch you some, yeah?

(JOHN *exits.* FRANK *takes his knife out and plays with it. He pretends to stab someone.* JOHN *enters and watches for a while, then at arm's length holds out the cake.*)

FRANK	What else they sayin' about me then?
JOHN	Well they've got the Marines out on the moors . . .
FRANK	Yeah? How many?
JOHN	Dunno . . . a fair few I reckon . . .
FRANK	Yeah, well they're gonna need them . . . (*He stabs the air.*)
JOHN	(*holding out the cake*) Here's your cake, Frank . . .
FRANK	BASTARDS!
	(*He nearly swipes the cake out of* JOHN'S *hands.*)
JOHN	You better take that off . . .
FRANK	What?
JOHN	Your mask.
FRANK	Eh?
JOHN	If you want to eat your cake.
FRANK	Yeah. Do you wanna try it on?
JOHN	No, no, you're alright . . .
FRANK	Go on . . .
JOHN	Na . . . I'll fix us both another drink . . .
FRANK	Go on . . . I wanna see what it looks like . . . 'ere . . .
	(*He puts it roughly on* JOHN'S *head.*)
FRANK	Well do somethin' then . . .

(JOHN *stands very still.*)

FRANK   Look like you're on the run . . . I know, come
               at me as if you're gonna rip me apart.

JOHN   No. Come on, just eat your cake, eh Frank?

FRANK   Go on, I wanna see it . . .

JOHN   But I can't even see proper . . .

FRANK   Come on . . . come at me . . . (*He slaps* JOHN's
               head playfully.)

JOHN   Give over, Frank, I can't even see where you
               are . . .

FRANK   (*slapping him harder*) Come on . . . what are
               you? A man or a bleedin' mouse? Shout
               somethin'!

JOHN   Shout what?

FRANK   Come on . . . come at me shouting. You're
               gonna kill me . . .

JOHN   I don't think this is a good idea, Frank.

FRANK   Come on, John, I wanna see what it looks like.

               (JOHN *takes off the mask.*)

JOHN   Look Frank, keep it down, eh? Keep it down,
               mate. We've got to watch it you know, we
               don't want to be heard next door.

               (*He hands back the mask.*)

FRANK   Did you smell 'er? Sniff it, 'ere sniff that bit.
               You can smell 'er perfume?

               (JOHN *reluctantly smells it.*)

How many bastard Marines do you reckon are out there then?

JOHN   Quite a few I reckon . . .

FRANK   A few hundred, yeah? (*He keeps smelling the mask and breathing deeply.*)

JOHN   Possibly . . .

FRANK   A few thousand even?

JOHN   Er, well . . . yeah, yeah maybe . . .

FRANK   I bet my family can't believe it.

JOHN   No . . . no, I bet they can't.

FRANK   What they sayin' again? (*He walks towards the mirror.*)

JOHN   (*puzzled*) Well . . .

FRANK   You know, what they callin' me?

JOHN   Oh. Britain's Most Dangerous Man . . .

FRANK   Britain's Most Dangerous Man. Yeah, I like that. (*He opens his mouth wide and looks at his teeth.*) I've got fantastic teeth, John, fuckin' amazing they are. Ron says I've got teeth like one of them movie stars. What do you think? (*He shows them.*)

JOHN   Yeah . . . great . . . fantastic, Frank . . .

FRANK   Do you reckon they're out there, John? With packs of dogs and torches and loaded guns? (JOHN's *not with him.*) Just like in that film. You've seen it, they all go after him, hundreds of 'em. But he's too quick for 'em, they can't even get near him . . .

JOHN   Who?

FRANK   The monster. The one with the bolt through his neck.

JOHN   Oh, you mean in Frankenstein, yeah. Frankenstein, I see . . .

FRANK   'Cos they all know, see . . .

JOHN   Know what?

FRANK   That he ain't like them . . .

JOHN   No, don't suppose he is.

FRANK   They can whip and torture him, even chain him up but it ain't never gonna keep him from escaping, they know that see. All the bastards that tried to keep me banged up, but the Governor, right, he knows there was no use. I 'ad to get out. I was with a working party on the moors, see. They let me run loose a bit, feed the wild ponies and that. It's wrong banging someone up without 'em knowing when they're gonna be free — ain't it?

JOHN   Yeah. Yeah, it is, Frank . . .

FRANK   Ron knows I done my time . . .

JOHN   (*trying to lighten things*) Yeah mate, well you're out now.

FRANK   So let 'em just try and catch me, I'd kill 'em, I'd kill anyone what tried to make me go back. I'm out now, ain't I? That's showin' 'em, ain't it? Me an' Ron, right, we've got big plans, see, we're gonna show them bastards no fucker can catch me, no one.

JOHN   I bet you're starvin', ain't you? I tell you, Frank, this steak is so fucking big it ain't gonna even fit on the plate . . .

FRANK Good, I like steak. Medium rare, just enough blood. (*He poses in the mirror.*) See this? (*Sticks his chest out.*) Just look at it, solid muscle that is, solid like a rock, like bleedin' iron. (*He punches his chest, stuffs cake into his mouth.*) Nine years I was banged up, nine fuckin' years. No fucker's gonna make me go back, no one, 'cos I'd kill 'em John, I'd have to. I'd kill anyone, I would, anyone, even you, John. (*He grins.*) Is there any more of that cake?

Scene Two

3:00 AM. Day two.

JOHN *is asleep on the settee. He gradually wakes to find* FRANK *standing over him with the knife.* FRANK *is restless, he can't sleep.* JOHN *is nervous.*

JOHN (*calmly*) Frank . . . (*Realising.*) Jesus Christ, mate, what you bleedin' doin'?

FRANK When they comin'?

JOHN No one's comin' now mate, it's the middle of the night. Why don't you get some rest, eh?

FRANK Me and Ron, right . . . we've got big plans . . .

JOHN Yeah . . . yeah . . . but you should really try and get some sleep . . .

FRANK We're gonna move to the country, see . . . just me and Ron, live in a big house an' that . . . and he promised, right, he promised I could keep lots of animals an' that . . .

JOHN (*still aware of the knife*) That's great . . . smashing . . . that's brilliant, Frank.

FRANK	Animals like mice and kittens and baby birds an' that . . . little ones, see, I like the little ones best.
JOHN	That's good. . . . little animals . . . that's nice . . .
FRANK	And Ron reckons that it'd be like a farm, see.
JOHN	A farm, yeah? Good, great . . . that's real nice, Frank.
FRANK	Yeah, and with some proper animals like sheep and cows, even lambs an' that . . . and we'd have a tractor and everythin'. And I'd be his right-hand man, see. I'll be doin' all the big jobs, 'cos I've got it sorted see, when I was inside I worked it all out. 'Course I could have me family to stay, anytime they wanted, but they'd 'ave to know, see, that at any time, right, I might 'ave to go out on a big job an' that, out the country even. So I reckon I'd have to show 'em all how to look after the animals, don't you?
JOHN	Yeah, oh yeah, definitely . . .
FRANK	'Cos I could be gone days, weeks even . . . 'cos I mean this house, right, it's gonna be our home, see, mine and Ron's, but that don't mean we ain't got the business to run. I tell you, I'm gonna be his right-hand man, John.
JOHN	Yeah . . . I know, Frank.
FRANK	He gave me that radio.
JOHN	Yeah, it's smart, Frank.
FRANK	. . . used to write to me an' that.
JOHN	That's good.
FRANK	Yeah, and I wrote back.

JOHN   So I bet you're shattered, ain't you?

FRANK   (*with sudden concern*) Ron and Reggie reckon
                I've got to write some letters to the papers an'
                that.

JOHN   Yeah, I know, they'll do the trick though,
                Frank, get everyone on your side.

FRANK   I was promised see, by the Governor, if I kept
                me head down, behaved myself an' that, he'd
                get me a parole date, and I trusted him, John.
                I believed that bastard, but he lied. The
                bastard was conning me all along, and Ron
                knows that, Ron knows the bastard lied. So
                where the fuck is he? Why ain't Ron been?

JOHN   He'll come soon, Frank, as soon as he can.

FRANK   I gotta see him. We've got big plans, see . . .

JOHN   Yeah, well, tomorrow we'll start on the
                letters, Frank. Get 'em sent off to all the big
                papers. Look, why don't you go back to bed,
                eh? Get some rest . . . it's your first big day of
                freedom tomorrow, I'll do you a massive fry-
                up special . . .

FRANK   Yeah. I'd like that . . . I like eggs. (*Playing
                with the knife.*) I 'ad me own budgie inside
                you know . . .

JOHN   . . . and then we can make a start on those
                letters . . .

FRANK   They let me keep him.

JOHN   I bet that double bed's a luxury, ain't it
                Frank?

FRANK   I called him Frank.

JOHN   Right . . .

FRANK	You know, after Frank Sinatra.
JOHN	Frank Sinatra. That's nice . . . good . . . that's great . . .
FRANK	When can I see my family?
JOHN	Soon . . . real soon . . .
FRANK	I wanna see my mother, tell her about the farm an' that . . .
JOHN	Yeah, well, first things first, eh? Letters to the papers, then we'll see, yeah?
FRANK	Do ya think Ron'll come tomorrow?
JOHN	Frank . . . Frank. . . . maybe it's better if I looked after the knife, eh? You know, for safety reasons, seeing as I'm out 'ere . . . yeah?
FRANK	You've got a gun, ain't you?
JOHN	Well, yeah.
FRANK	Do you wanna swap?
JOHN	No! No, no you're alright . . . you get some rest, eh?
	(*A beat.*)
FRANK	You ever 'ad a budgie, John?
JOHN	No . . . well, I'm not very good with animals.
FRANK	They're always looking in their little mirrors, see, John.
JOHN	Yeah?
FRANK	Yeah, trying to work it out . . . he's working out why that other bird keeps on staring at him.

JOHN　　　　Right.

FRANK　　　I should have let him fly away . . . but I
thought he'd miss him . . .

JOHN　　　　Miss who?

FRANK　　　The other one. In the mirror . . . I think he
loved him, see . . .

JOHN　　　　Oh, right, yeah, yeah . . . I see, the other bird
in the mirror, nice.

FRANK　　　I was trying to tell him . . . explain I was
going away . . . I was stroking his little head
but he was a stupid little fucker, Frankie, only
'ad a little brain, see. I was only tellin' him I
was gonna let him fly away, but he made me
squeeze him too tight. 'Cos he looked so
scared . . . his little eyes looked so scared,
John, so I 'ad to squeeze him to keep him safe,
but it was too tight, see, and I squeezed the
life out of him, John. I killed Frankie.

JOHN　　　　Shit, that's a shame.

FRANK　　　His little eyes came right out, John, both of
'em, tiny little things.

JOHN　　　　Fuck.

FRANK　　　I've still got him . . .

JOHN　　　　Eh?

FRANK　　　He's in my pocket, do you wanna see him?

JOHN　　　　Well . . .

(FRANK *reaches into his pocket and cupping
his hands moves forward to show* JOHN, *then
opens his hands. They're empty.*)

FRANK   I had you going, didn't I? (*Beat. Then almost
                  in a whisper.*) Na, John, he's under me pilla'.

                            Scene Three

The following morning. JOHN *is clearing up the mess caused
by* FRANK *showing off to Reg and the boys. They've just left
and* FRANK *is acting like an over-excited child.*

FRANK   I showed 'em all, didn't I? I showed Reg and
                  the boys . . . did you see their faces? They
                  were amazed John, they couldn't believe how
                  strong I am, and that fuckin' paddy, I nearly
                  broke 'is bleedin' arm. I could 'ave John, I
                  could have snapped it clean off. I tell you,
                  they couldn't believe how strong I am . . . and
                  Reg, right, did you see how he didn't really
                  want a go, I tell you it's 'cos he knows, see,
                  he knows I'm the best fuckin' arm wrestler, he
                  didn't want them to see me beat him. Yeah, I
                  tell you John, not one of 'em stood a bleedin'
                  chance, not one of them could beat me, I'm
                  the fuckin' best arm wrestler in Britain.
                  (*Pretends to wrestle.*) Wham . . . easy . . .
                  fuckin' easy meat.

JOHN   Right, Frank . . .

FRANK   Did you see 'is fuckin' face, John? (*Laughs.*)

JOHN   Right then, Frank, you heard what the twins
                  want, I'll fetch some paper so you can make a
                  start on them letters to the papers, yeah?

FRANK   (*in a world of his own*) Did you see me? Did
                  you see me take Reg on? He's strong as well
                  you know, but this arm's me killing arm, see.
                  Powerful, see this grip, right, it's like a
                  bleedin' vice, John.

JOHN   Yeah, yeah, so I'll fetch the paper, make a
                  start on those letters, yeah?

FRANK   Inside I could do anyone you know, easy . . .
fuckin' no problem. I tell you John, I was a
champion amongst men . . .

JOHN   I can imagine . . .

FRANK   See, Ron knows that . . . He'll piss his-self
when Reg tells him he took me on . . . best
fuckin' arm wrestler in Britain, he reckons,
easy. Fuckin' easy, John . . .

JOHN   Yeah, yeah, great, Frank, brilliant . . .
champion amongst men, eh? Fantastic Frank,
but you know what you've gotta do now, yeah?

FRANK   . . . and Reg, right, well, he ain't bad himself
you know, but you see, he ain't like Ron, he's
a fuckin' loser on his own, he won't do
anything without Ron, see. He loses, he's
fuckin' weak, see. Now if Ron 'ad been 'ere —
but he knows me and Ron, we're like this
tight, see, real close, and we've got plans. He
should 'ave known I just can't be beaten,
John. I reckon he don't like it either, you
know? Did you see his face, John? I wish Ron
'ad been 'ere, he knows, see, Ron knows I
ain't never been beaten, it's as simple as that.
You ever arm wrestled with Ron?

JOHN   No, no, can't say I have . . . so . . .

FRANK   Course you do know I taught Ron all he
knows, 'bout arm wrestling an' that. I tell you
John, when we were in Wandsworth together
we used to arm wrestle all the time. Oh yeah, I
gave him a few good tips, like never let go,
and stare the bastard out, it unnerves them,
see. Course it's a lot more than that, it's the
power of the mind, see, you've got to know
you can do it, you've got to know you can beat
them, and I ain't never been beaten John,
never.

JOHN   We'll eat, then make a start on these letters, eh?

FRANK   (*sitting down, ready to arm wrestle*) Sure you don't wanna try your luck, John?

JOHN   Me? Oh no . . . no, no thanks, I need me arms in one piece, mate. I've got potatoes to peel, and you've got those letters to write, Frank.

FRANK   Yeah. Eh, you should have seen your face when I lifted you up by your belt . . . fuckin' brilliant it was. I bet you couldn't believe it, eh? One fuckin' arm. Easy. Inside I done two, one each arm. I think Reg was impressed. 'Ere, John, his fuckin' face when I picked that fat bloke up, did you see him sweat? He was sweating like a bleedin' pig.

JOHN   Yeah, he was Frank

FRANK   Yeah. (*Laughs.*) Like a bleedin' fat pig. (*Goes to mirror, looks at himself.*) Do you think I look like Tarzan?

JOHN   Yeah . . . yeah, you do, Frank.

FRANK   Yeah . . . I reckon I do as well. (*He does the Tarzan yell.*)

(*A musical set piece follows with four tableaux:* 1. JOHN *holds up a letter for* FRANK *to copy;* 2. FRANK *makes a mistake and screws up paper;* 3. JOHN *waits expectantly.* FRANK *finishes writing. Gestures of triumph from* JOHN; 4. *Both reading newspapers, find* FRANK'S *letter and rejoice.*)

Scene Four

Later. JOHN and FRANK playing cards. FRANK throws cards into the air.

FRANK   I'm sick of bleedin' cards . . . I only beat you anyway . . .

JOHN   Yeah. (*Sarcastic.*) You're too good for me, Frank . . .

FRANK   Jesus, John, when's something gonna happen?

JOHN   You just gotta sit tight, Frank.

FRANK   But why ain't they doin' anything?

JOHN   I told you, Frank, things ain't that simple. Ron's laying low himself, he's up against it, you know . . . the bloke's doin' his best . . .

FRANK   I don't understand it, John, why ain't they done anything? Why didn't the fuckin' letter work? Ron said that's what I had to do. He said they'd 'ave to take notice then.

JOHN   They printed it mate, they know the score. It's just the Home Secretary, Frank. He's the arsehole, he's the one that's fuckin' things up. But you give it time, I tell you he'll come round . . . you wait and see.

FRANK   Yeah, 'cos it was a good letter, wasn't it?

JOHN   It was a great letter, it was the business, Frank.

FRANK   They gotta take notice, ain't they, John? Ron said they would, so they gotta, ain't they?

JOHN   Yeah, they will, Frank, just trust us, eh?

FRANK   Yeah, they gotta . . . so how long?

JOHN   Soon, Frank.

FRANK   How long's fuckin' soon, John?

JOHN   Look, Frank, you've gotta take it easy, you
                know . . . relax, take a bath . . . do your
                exercises . . . play a few cards . . . but stay
                calm, eh? If Reg comes by and sees you wound
                up, well it ain't gonna please 'im, is it?
                They're doing everything for you, you know?
                They ain't gonna take kindly to you throwing
                it in their faces . . . you gotta show them that
                you're happy, Frank. You're out now and soon
                things are gonna be going your way, remember
                what Ron promised . . . nice house, plenty of
                money . . . yeah? Trust us. It's gonna be great
                Frank, it's gonna be sweet, you know . . .

FRANK   I can't sit down no more, John . . . I can't . . .
                I can't sit down, at least inside they let me out
                . . . I could work on the moors, John . . . feed
                the ponies . . . I could get out . . . this is
                worse . . . this ain't free, is it? This is worse
                than fuckin' prison

JOHN   You know that ain't true, Frank, you know
                you've had steak every night, and it's no
                ordinary steak, we're talking saw off the horns
                and wipe its arse, we're talking as much booze
                as you like. Jesus, Frank, you know you can
                have anything you want.

                (*Long pause.*)

FRANK   Yeah, well I want a woman. I wanna fuck a
                woman. (*He kicks off.*) Or else I'm gonna go
                and get me own. Tell him, John, tell him I've
                gotta fuck . . . I've gotta fuck a woman. I want
                one now, ring him.

JOHN   I can't ring him just like that —

FRANK   Right then, I will . . . (*He grabs the phone,
                stops and looks at* JOHN.) Shit, what's his
                bleedin' number?

JOHN   Give me the phone, Frank . . .

FRANK   I wanna talk to Ron. I wanna tell him I want a
                 woman.

JOHN   Alright . . . I know . . . but let me do it, eh?

FRANK   (*frustrated*) I wanna speak to Ron!

JOHN   Why don't you have that bath, eh, Frank?

FRANK   My legs won't fit in it proper, they're too big.
                 They're too fuckin' big, John . . .

JOHN   I'll make you a couple of boiled eggs, yeah?

FRANK   Will you cut the bread up?

JOHN   Yeah, I will. You go take a nice bath and I'll
                 fix you some eggs.

FRANK   Six, John. I want six — not too hard, not too
                 soft . . . bread cut into soldiers, put around the
                 egg like the sun. Tell him I'll be real gentle . . .
                 I won't hurt her, tell him I'll be real nice to
                 her an' that.

JOHN   Who?

FRANK   The woman. The blonde. (*A sudden demand.*)
                 She's gotta be blonde.

                         Scene Five

JOHN *on the telephone to Reg.*

JOHN   Yeah, yeah, well he seems to think he can
                 have anything he wants. I mean I told him,
                 you know, I said he's bleedin' lucky to be out,
                 but he won't have it, he wants a woman. I
                 don't know, I suppose he's been banged up a
                 long time. Yeah. Yeah, well he don't think
                 like us, does he? He gets a fuckin' idea into
                 his head and won't let go. Well, if you ask me
                 we've got no choice, he's threatening to go

and find one . . . Course not, fuck no . . .
Well, he does his exercises and gets fuckin'
all wound up. I tell you the bloke groans all
night long. Yeah, fit to fuckin' burst . . . well
it might just calm him down a bit . . . fuck
knows . . . couple of nights? . . . Sweet, yeah,
yeah . . . I'll tell him. Yeah . . . He just misses
his family. I know, I know it's hard to believe
but I tell you the crazy bastard even reckons
that Ron's promised 'im a big house in the
country somewhere, eh? Fuck, I never said —
well, yeah, I know he, Reg, I never said,
course he's a man of his word. Yeah, yeah —
I didn't mean — no I can handle it, no sweat,
no problem — yeah, I'll tell him, Reg, trust
me — alright, yes, fuck, I'm sorry, alright?
Yes I know, well he said it was Ron's idea.
Yeah, yeah . . . no, I won't say anything, come
on, I'm not that stupid . . . yeah. (*Puts the
phone down.*) Jesus Christ, what did I say?

Scene Six

The following day. FRANK *and* JOHN *are playing cards.*

FRANK   What time is it?

JOHN   'Bout five minutes later than the last time you
                 asked.

FRANK   (*looking at the phone*) It is working, ain't it?

JOHN   Yeah, yeah, you in again?

FRANK   Na . . . so what time did they say again?

JOHN   Ten, eleven . . . midnight, two in the morning,
                 you know how it is . . .

FRANK   What colour hair?

JOHN   Blonde, brunette, red head, does it matter?

FRANK   Course it matters, I want a blonde one . . .

JOHN   Don't we all . . .

FRANK   You did tell 'em, didn't you?

JOHN   Yeah, yeah . . .

FRANK   Blonde, yeah?

JOHN   Blonde . . . yeah . . .

FRANK   And what?

JOHN   I'm not with you, mate.

FRANK   And what the fuck did they say?

JOHN   You know what they said, they said "Give the crazy bastard what he wants."

FRANK   And she'll be blonde?

JOHN   Look, Frank. I told them straight, "blonde". I said "not too tall, not too small, nice figure, nice face, nice voice". Right?

FRANK   Yeah, good, right . . . what time is it?

JOHN   Look, Frank, why don't you take a bath? Eh? Calm yourself?

FRANK   Why?

JOHN   Calm yourself.

FRANK   Are you sayin' I smell?

JOHN   I'm sayin' it might relax you, alright?

FRANK   So I don't smell?

JOHN   Frank, how can you possibly smell, mate, you spend half the day in the bleedin' bathroom.

FRANK	Do I look good?
JOHN	Yeah, yeah, you look smart, you look the bleedin' business. Alright?
FRANK	Fit an' that? Do I look fit an' that? (*He poses.*)
JOHN	Yeah, solid, well impressive . . .
FRANK	What about teeth?
JOHN	Yeah, you've got great teeth . . .
FRANK	They clean an' that?
JOHN	Yeah, they're clean an' that . . .
FRANK	(*he smells his breath*) You sure?
JOHN	Frank, your teeth are beautiful, mate. I mean I can see my bleedin' face in them. Calm down and have a game, eh?
FRANK	So they're gonna ring first? Yeah? You know, to say they're on their way, yeah? I mean what's the score then? Is it a ring we answer or a ring we ignore?
JOHN	Yeah, yeah, they're gonna ring first, two rings, no need to answer, easy . . . so my deal . . .
	(*He deals the cards.* FRANK *paces up and down the room.*)
FRANK	And the girl, right? The blonde, are they gonna bring 'er with them?
JOHN	Probably.
FRANK	Good . . . wait a minute, you said probably.

JOHN   Did I?

FRANK   So what the fuck does that mean?

JOHN   It means probably . . .

FRANK   But does that mean yes?

JOHN   It means probably, Frank . . .

FRANK   But does that mean yes?

JOHN   Bleedin' 'ell Frank . . . YES, alright, it means
                yes . . . so sit down and play the game, eh?

FRANK   (*in thought*) It don't mean yes . . . it means
                nothing like yes . . . why did you say probably
                if it means no . . .

JOHN   Alright Frank . . . definitely . . . they are
                definitely bringing the girl with them, alright?
                Is that definite enough for you? Can I spell it
                out a bit more? Frank, play the game, eh?

FRANK   Yes or fuckin' no?

JOHN   Frank. You want a blonde, right? I want you
                to have a blonde, and you know the twins want
                you to have a blonde, so why don't we play a
                few cards and bleedin' wait, eh?

                (FRANK *pulls a face.*)

JOHN   Frank, listen to me, you're bleedin' lucky to
                be here, you know.

FRANK   So what the bleedin' 'ell does that mean? Shit,
                she ain't blonde, is she?

JOHN   It means let it drop, right?

FRANK   Let it drop?

JOHN   Yeah, I've had enough Frank, I'm sick of your
                stupid fuckin' demands, you know?

FRANK   You called me stupid!

JOHN   Frank, come on, mate. We're both a bit edgy
               you know, cooped up in this place day and
               night, but the girl's gonna be here soon, so
               just let it drop.

FRANK   I ain't fuckin' stupid.

JOHN   No? Well, wise up then.

               (*The phone rings.*)

FRANK   Shit . . . they're on their way . . . Fuck, John,
               they're coming . . . shit, where are they? (*He
               looks around.*)

JOHN   Cool it, they'll be a while yet. 'Ere. (*Handing
               him a drink.*)

FRANK   No . . . the chocolates, where's the fuckin'
               chocolates?

               (JOHN *hands him the chocolates. He smells
               them.*)

FRANK   I hope they're fresh . . .

JOHN   Course they're fresh . . .

FRANK   Half white, half black, right?

JOHN   Milk and plain . . . yes.

               (FRANK *sits, clutching the chocolates.*)

JOHN   Frank, if you keep handling them they're
               gonna melt, mate.

FRANK   Shit . . . (*He puts them down.*) Do you think
               they have?

JOHN   No, no, they'll be fine. Shall we have another
               round?

FRANK   No . . . no . . . do you think she'll like 'em?
                 The chocolates, do you think she'll like 'em,
                 John?

JOHN   She'll love 'em . . .

FRANK   I wonder which she'll like best . . . ?

JOHN   She'll love them all, Frank.

FRANK   I wonder what she's called, John.

JOHN   I wonder if she can cook . . .

FRANK   Why?

JOHN   Why do you think?

FRANK   She ain't here to bleedin' cook!

JOHN   No, I was joking . . .

FRANK   I don't want 'er bleedin' cookin'.

JOHN   Frank, it was a joke . . .

FRANK   (*in thought*) I wonder what she smells of.

JOHN   Smells of?

FRANK   Yeah . . . they all smell different, don't they?

JOHN   Yeah, I suppose they do.

FRANK   (*matter of fact*) Shit, John. I hope she's a
                 blonde, I've never fucked a blonde one before.

                 (*The doorbell rings. They look at each other.*)

FRANK   Oh fuck . . .

JOHN   Jesus, that was bleedin' quick.

FRANK   Go on . . . go on, John . . . wait . . .

                 (*The bell rings again.*)

FRANK   It's them, it's them, John.

JOHN	Stay in the bedroom till I give you the all clear . . . Frank?
FRANK	John? Stand or sit . . .
JOHN	What?
FRANK	Stand or sit? When she comes in, shall I stand like this, right, or sit here like this?
JOHN	Frank, it might not be them . . .
	(*The bell rings again.*)
FRANK	It is . . . I know it . . . shit, John, she's here . . . what do you think?
JOHN	Frank, you better get in the bedroom, just in case . . .
FRANK	No, I wanna see her, the minute she walks in I wanna see her, I wanna see her face and the way she walks. Fuck, John, do you think she'll like me?
JOHN	(*smiles*) Definitely, Frank. She'll bleedin' love you, mate . . .

(JOHN *exits to the door and* FRANK *is left alone. He checks his breath, smells the chocolates and stares at the door. He stands, then sits. Then stands again. Takes his mask out of his pocket and considers wearing it, then changes his mind and thrusts out his chest. He looks ridiculous.*)

Scene Seven

3:00 AM. Day six.

FRANK *and* LISA, *a brunette 'hostess', are sitting drinking tea. There is a slight awkward tension as* FRANK *tries hard to impress and make conversation.*

FRANK   Do you want another cup of tea, Lisa?

LISA   No thanks, this is fine, thanks.

FRANK   What about the radio?

LISA   Sorry?

FRANK   Do you want the radio on?

LISA   No, no, you're alright . . .

FRANK   Because I do have my own radio.

LISA   That's nice.

FRANK   I brought it with me, see . . .

           (LISA *just looks at him and nods and smiles
           tightly.*)

FRANK   When I escaped an' that . . .

           (*She does the same again.*)

           'Cos I escaped from Dartmoor, see . . .

LISA   Yes, I know.

FRANK   It was on the news, in all the papers an' that.
           I even wrote a letter to the *Times* and the
           fuckin' *Mirror* an' that, did you see it?

LISA   No . . . no, I didn't.

FRANK   They had thousands of Marines out on the
           moors.

           (LISA *nods and smiles.*)

FRANK   With hundreds of vicious fuckin' dogs.

LISA   Oh . . .

FRANK   'Cept they never caught me . . .

LISA   No. (*Smiles.*) I can see.

FRANK   'Cos I was already here, see. (*Pause.*) Ron
            gave me the radio.

LISA   That's kind.

FRANK   He sprung me, you know, from Dartmoor.

LISA   Yes . . . I know.

FRANK   We've got big plans, see . . . you know, me
            and Ron.

LISA   Oh. . . . good.

FRANK   Do you want another cup of tea?

LISA   No . . . oh, alright then, thanks. (*He pours her
            tea.*) Look, how long do you think John'll be?

FRANK   I don't know, we've had cake . . . 'cept it's all
            gone.

LISA   You don't mind waiting do you, Frank?

            (*Pause.*)

FRANK   You called me Frank.

LISA   (*smiles*) Well that's your name, isn't it?

FRANK   Yeah . . . it sounds nice. . . . you know, when
            you say it.

            (*Pause.*)

LISA   Frank?

FRANK   See . . . it's nice . . . you say it nice.

LISA	Do you mind waiting, until John gets back? It's just, well, I do have to make sure I get my money . . . you understand, don't you?
FRANK	Lisa . . .
LISA	Yes?
FRANK	It's a nice name, Lisa, it's nice . . .
LISA	Thanks. So's Frank.
FRANK	I had a budgie called Frank.
LISA	Same as you, eh?
FRANK	Eh? Oh no, after Frank Sinatra.
LISA	Oh . . . I see. . . . that's nice.
FRANK	Don't you like your chocolates?
LISA	Yeah, they're lovely, Frank.
FRANK	Black and white.
LISA	Sorry?
FRANK	They're both see, black and white, both. One lot are black and the other lot are white, one's on top and the other's underneath, I think. I didn't know which you liked the best so I got you both, in one box an' that . . . it's clever really, you know, putting both in one box, they ain't cheap ones neither . . .
LISA	No, I can see . . .
FRANK	Are you goin' to open them?
LISA	Well I'd rather save them if you don't mind.

FRANK   No . . . no, that's alright, 'cos they are fresh. I
        mean they'll probably keep right up to
        Christmas Day even.

LISA   (*smiles*) Oh right, well, maybe I'll open them
        on Christmas Day then.

FRANK   My mother's called Gladys . . . I'm going to
        clean my teeth.

LISA   Oh . . . right . . . okay.

        (LISA *has a few moments by herself. A chance
        for us to really see her face. She's relaxed,
        professional. After a time* JOHN *enters.*)

JOHN   Where is he? Bathroom?

LISA   Yeah . . . (*She looks at the bag he's holding.*)

JOHN   Doin' his teeth, right?

LISA   Yes . . . did you get it?

JOHN   Yes I got it . . . one hundred notes. I . . . I
        took my cut like they said, twenty, right for
        my expenses and that . . .

LISA   Twenty?

JOHN   I'm 'ere, ain't I?

LISA   What's that got to do with me?

JOHN   Well, I cook an' that . . .

LISA   I can do my own cooking thanks.

JOHN   You're not here to cook . . .

LISA   (*ignoring him*) Two days they said, right?

JOHN   . . . and you want protection, don't you?

LISA   From you? (*She laughs.*)

JOHN   Look, darlin', we're both here to do a job,
              right? Mine's to see he don't go hungry and
              yours is to make sure he don't go without . . .
              alright? Hey and don't you worry, Lisa, I ain't
              scared of Frankie Boy . . .

              (FRANK *walks in wearing his mask.*)

JOHN   Fuck!

FRANK   (*taking it off*) I made it myself.

LISA   Right, Frank, are you gonna show me the way?

              (FRANK *looks at her. A beat.*)

LISA   To the bedroom.

              (FRANK *follows then turns back to* JOHN.)

FRANK   This is better than a blonde, John.

JOHN   Definitely, Frank.

                          Scene Eight

Day seven.

FRANK *and* LISA *are having sex, off. It's loud but short-lived.*
JOHN *is listening to the racing on the radio. It's nearing the*
winning post. Both scenes blend together. LISA *enters to one*
side and is sick into a bucket. LISA *enters the lounge.* JOHN
clicks his lamp on.

LISA   Oh . . . I didn't see you there.

JOHN   No, I know . . .

              (*They both listen for sounds from* FRANK.)

LISA   He must have dropped off . . .

JOHN	Yeah . . .
LISA	Non-stop for two days. It feels like bleedin' weeks . . .
JOHN	Well what did you expect? For a bloke like Frank, nine years is a bleedin' long time.
LISA	Yeah? For a bloke like Frank nine minutes is a long time.
JOHN	I heard you.
LISA	I can imagine, I mean he nearly deafens me . . .
JOHN	In the bathroom. I heard you throwing up . . .
LISA	Oh . . .
JOHN	And it ain't my cookin', is it?
LISA	No, no, it isn't . . .
JOHN	So how far gone are you?
	(*Pause.*)
LISA	Enough.
JOHN	What you gonna do?
LISA	I'm doin' it.
JOHN	You mean the money?
LISA	Jesus, John, why else would I be here?
JOHN	Well, he ain't gonna know. I mean it doesn't show . . .
LISA	No? No, I don't suppose it does but me just knowing's enough . . .

JOHN   Yeah . . . and Christmas is coming . . . the
                goose is getting fat . . . money . . . we all need
                the money . . .

LISA   Oh.

JOHN   Can I get you anything when I go out?

LISA   No, no, you're alright. Well, I'll be going
                soon.

JOHN   It's no problem, I've got other things to get.

LISA   But I'll be going soon . . .

JOHN   Right.

LISA   I can go home, can't I, John?

JOHN   Yeah, course you can . . .

LISA   Tonight?

JOHN   Well, tonight's a bit tricky, Lisa.

LISA   What do you mean?

JOHN   I mean it's a bit tricky right now . . .

LISA   Don't muck me about, John . . . can I or can't
                I go home tonight?

JOHN   No.

LISA   (*angry now*) No?

JOHN   They want you to stay a bit longer. (*Laughs
                lightly.*) You're the only one that can calm
                him down.

LISA   Two days they said.

JOHN   I know, but . . . well, he's crazy about you.

LISA	Well that's not my problem. I'm sorry, John, but I can't.
JOHN	If you leave he'll only try and come after you.
LISA	Jesus, this isn't fair, John. Two days they said, I wouldn't have taken it if I'd known, I can't stay.
JOHN	Well are you gonna phone Ron and tell him?
	(*Pause.*)
LISA	So what you're really sayin' is I've got no choice.
JOHN	Well, it ain't that bad . . . stay a few more nights, and well, you could talk him into giving himself up.
LISA	Me?
JOHN	Like I said, he's crazy about you.
LISA	But is that what the twins want?
JOHN	(*ignoring her*) Drink?
LISA	John? Is that what Ron wants?
JOHN	Come on, Lisa, this is a no-win situation . . . this is back-against-the-wall, Frank, this is hello Mr Crazy Bastard . . .
LISA	What do you mean?
JOHN	The longer he's out the less chance he's got of getting what he wants and, think about it, he ain't gonna go back easy, he's got his big bleedin' plans, ain't he?
LISA	Oh, I don't know, John . . .

JOHN   Look, if he gives himself up now, and there's
             no trouble, well, he could get off lightly, they
             might go easy on him. He's not stupid. He
             knows this ain't freedom.

LISA   But is he gonna listen to me?

JOHN   You could try, make him think it's his idea.

LISA   But what does Ron say?

JOHN   Ron's got enough to worry about . . . if we
             handle Frank right, we're, well, sweet, you
             know. Look, stay and I'll see about upping
             your money. (*Pause.*) I know you like the
             bloke, Jesus, I'm fond of him meself, but he's
             a crazy bastard . . . keep 'im banged up in 'ere
             for too long and I tell you he's gonna kick off
             big time. Look we've got Christmas round the
             corner and other places we need to be . . . and
             I know you could do with the extra cash . . .

LISA   Yeah. Yeah, OK then, I'll stay. But I need two
             — I need at least two hundred.

                      Scene Nine

Later that evening. LISA *and* FRANK *on the sofa.*

LISA   John said it's snowing. I love the snow, don't
             you?

FRANK   When it's white I do.

LISA   (*laughs*) Snow is always white, Frank.

FRANK   It ain't, it can be mucky. In the yard it was
             always mucky.

LISA   Yeah, I suppose you're right. God, isn't it
             awful the way things never stay nice? It
             always gets ruined . . . spoiled. Why can't
             things just stay nice? I mean all that snow . . .

it makes everything seem really beautiful . . .
but then you're right, it gets all mucky and
slushy and before you know it it's gone. I
could never understand that, how something
so lovely can just disappear overnight . . .

FRANK   My old man worked in a slaughterhouse . . .
he killed cows for a living. Stun 'em, slash
'em, gut 'em, hang 'em. We've all got to die
some way . . .

LISA   Frank, I was thinking, well, maybe . . . maybe
you should think about giving yourself up . . .

FRANK   They call me the Mad Axe Man.

LISA   I know. Frank, did you hear what I said? I
think they might be ready to listen to you now
. . . Frank?

FRANK   Have you checked under the bed?

LISA   What?

FRANK   For the axe . . . have you checked under the
bed?

LISA   No . . . yes . . . please, Frank . . . I'm worried
about you, darling . . . I only want what's best
for you.

(FRANK *goes the table and begins writing.*)

FRANK   I'm only gonna do what Ron wants, and Ron's
got big plans.

LISA   Oh, I see . . .

FRANK   Anyway, I ain't never going back . . .

LISA   It would be nice to be a free man though,
wouldn't it? With a proper release date and
everything . . .

FRANK   They just lie . . . (*He makes a mistake.*) Shit.

LISA   What you doin'?

FRANK   Writing a letter.

LISA   A letter? Who to, Frank? Frank?

FRANK   What you looking at?

LISA   Your mouth, it's all over your mouth, look . . .
            come 'ere, you daft thing . . . it's ink, look.

            (*She wipes his mouth.*)

FRANK   It's this pen . . . look, it's a proper ink pen
            with real ink and that . . . see . . .

LISA   (*hesitant*) Who are you writing to?

FRANK   Lobsters have blue blood . . .

LISA   Frank, who's the letter to?

FRANK   Squids have ink sacks . . .

LISA   Come 'ere. It's all over your tongue . . .

FRANK   A chameleon's tongue is twice as long as its
            body . . .

LISA   Frank — who are you writing a letter to?

FRANK   They only change colour when they're scared.

LISA   Frank. Who's the letter to?

FRANK   No one . . . me mother. I'm inviting her to our
            party.

LISA   (*shocked*) Our party! Where?

FRANK   Here . . . I'm gonna ask John to take it round
            to her . . .

LISA   Does Reg know?

FRANK   I'm gonna send him and Ron one. (*Pause.*) If
                you cut a cockroach's head off very carefully,
                it'll still live, for weeks even.

LISA   Frank, what do you say, eh? 'Bout going back
                and me visiting you every week and writing to
                you.

FRANK   But if it's not looked after properly it'll starve
                to death.

LISA   (*snaps*) But how can you feed it, without its
                head?

FRANK   (*looking closely at her*) You can't . . .

LISA   (*distant*) But why would anyone want to cut its
                head off? Frank?

FRANK   To watch it die . . . We should get some of
                that cake? For the party. It's nice, you'll like
                it. 'Ere, we can get some hats, party hats,
                what do you think? Lisa?

                (LISA *is in a daze. She knows she cannot win.*)

LISA   Yeah . . . party hats . . . lovely, Frank . . .
                that's a great idea . . .

                              Scene Ten

JOHN *and* LISA, *a short time later. There is a sense of urgency.*

JOHN   Where is he now?

LISA   In the bathroom doing his teeth . . . Jesus,
                John, what are we going to do?

FRANK   A bleedin' party?

LISA   Yeah, a bleedin' party.

JOHN   Jesus, he'll be wanting to invite the family
over next . . . (*He sees her face.*) What? Shit
. . . where's his head at? Bleedin' 'ell, I tell
you, Lisa, this is just the start. Now he thinks
he's on his bleedin' holidays . . . he does, I
tell you the guy is losing it, he is . . . big
fuckin' time. He thinks it's happy families
'ere. Jesus, can you see it . . . can you? Ronnie
and Reg in bleedin' party hats eating flamin'
cake . . . Jesus Christ, Lisa, the guy has lost
it.

LISA   He just doesn't understand, John.

FRANK   Understand? (*Laughs.*) What is there to
bleedin' understand? He's an escaped criminal
. . . The bleedin' Mad Axe Man. For fuck's
sake, Lisa, he thinks he's Tarzan and he's
still got a bleedin' knife.

LISA   Shhh! He might hear us.

JOHN   And what's all this cleaning his teeth for, eh?
It ain't normal, the bloke must clean his
bleedin' teeth a hundred times a day . . .
What's that about, eh? I tell you what, he's
lost it.

LISA   I don't think he's the only one . . .

(*Pause.* JOHN *looks at her.*)

JOHN   I'm not the one who winds the fucker up.

LISA   No? So are you sayin' I am? I thought I was
the only one who could calm him? Look, if
that's the case then I might as well walk out
that door now.

JOHN   (*panic*) NO! . . . No . . . no, you are . . . Jesus,
Lisa, you're doin' a great job . . . The twins
right, they told me to tell you you're doin' a

great job . . . fantastic . . . They're well
pleased . . . well pleased . . . he just . . . he
just makes me nervous, you know . . . all this
talk about parties . . . fuck . . . (*Laughs.*)
Where's his head at, eh?

LISA   So what are you going to do?

JOHN   Me? Do? . . . I've got a gun.

(*She looks at him.*)

(*half-laugh*) I could always blow my fuckin'
brains out.

LISA   Christ, John . . . Just don't let Frank see it . . .

JOHN   They'll be ringin' soon and what then? Jesus,
he's gonna hear it and be out here . . . he's
gonna be out here inviting the whole bleedin'
Firm to his party.

LISA   He might be in the bath now.

JOHN   Party hats . . . fuckin' party hats, I ask you.

(FRANK *enters.*)

FRANK   What time they ringing?

JOHN   Eh?

FRANK   Reg — what time's he ringing?

LISA   Oh . . . er . . . they already have, Frank . . .

FRANK   Did you tell 'em 'bout my party?

JOHN   Er . . . yeah . . . no . . . look, Frank . . .

LISA   I . . . I wanted an early night . . . just me and
you . . . kind of special, John's gonna get
some cake and we're gonna have our own
little party . . . just the two of us . . . in bed.

Yeah? Frank? You can have them round
another night, but tonight's gonna be just ours
. . . well? Shall we get started?

(FRANK *and* LISA *look at* JOHN.)

JOHN   Yeah, I'll go and get the gear then . . .

LISA   Frank? What sort of party games do you fancy,
eh?

FRANK   (*turning to* JOHN) Don't forget the hats . . .

(*They exit to the bedroom.* JOHN *watches them
go.*)

Scene Eleven

LISA *is lying on the sofa.* FRANK *is doing press-ups.*

LISA   Frank, it's the middle of the night . . .

FRANK   How many is that?

LISA   Twenty . . . five or somethin' — I don't know.
Frank, come back to bed, I want to talk to
you . . .

FRANK   Count out loud . . .

LISA   Frank, please listen to me . . . I'm worried
about you, I am. Frank, I really think you
should give yourself up . . .

FRANK   You're not counting . . .

LISA   I'm scared things'll go wrong, Frank . . . I'm
scared they'll find you and what then? You
won't have any choice, they'll make you go
back . . .

FRANK

I've told you I ain't goin' back. See this muscle, right? Just look at it, Lisa, solid as a rock. Feel it, go on. Solid as a bleedin' rock.

LISA

Yeah, I know, Frank. If you leave it any longer and they find you they'll really come down hard on you . . . You know?

(*He ignores her.*)

LISA

But if you gave yourself up without any bother, well they'd see you're no big threat, they'd see you're not really a danger — they might still give you an early release date, Frank . . .

FRANK

See these teeth right, name any film star and I've got teeth as good as them, it's true, any. Go on, name one . . .

LISA

Frank, why won't you listen to me?

FRANK

Bob Hope, Bing Crosby, even . . . Tarzan.

LISA

You know I'm right, don't you?

FRANK

Don't you think I look like Tarzan?

LISA

Frank, please . . .

FRANK

Ron, right, Ron is always saying that, you know, he is. Oh yeah, well not just Ron either. I tell you everyone says it, they all say I look like a movie star, it's a fact . . . 'tis, it's a solid gold fact, I mean just look at this face Lisa, fuckin' star quality or what?

LISA

Yeah, Frank . . . it's star quality . . .

FRANK

Don't you think I look like Tarzan?

LISA

Yeah, you do . . . Frank, will you listen to me . . . I mean it . . . I'm really worried about you.

FRANK   I'm not ever going back.

LISA   (*angry*) Stop saying that, it's . . . stupid.

FRANK   (*suddenly serious*) I ain't bleedin' stupid,
             what's wrong with you? Ain't they payin' you
             enough?

LISA   What do you mean?

FRANK   Well they are payin' you, aren't they?

LISA   I don't care about the money . . . I care about
             you . . .

FRANK   How much they payin' you?

LISA   I don't know . . . Frank, don't . . .

FRANK   Hundred up front, wasn't it?

LISA   Well . . . no, it was eighty actually . . .

FRANK   So what's that then?

LISA   What do you mean?

FRANK   How much each fuck?

LISA   Don't say that . . .

FRANK   Why? It's true, ain't it? You do fuck for
             money, don't you?

LISA   It's not like that . . .

FRANK   So what we been doin' then?

LISA   I care about you, Frank . . .

FRANK   What we been doin', Lisa? Come on, tell me . . .

             (*He pushes her onto the sofa.*)

LISA	I'm not listening to this . . . you're not gonna spoil things . . .
FRANK	Shall I show you? (*He moves closer to her and starts to undo his belt.*)
LISA	Alright, if that's what you want . . . show me . . . come on, then . . . I'M READY, COME ON!
FRANK	(*quietly*) I want you to say it, I just want you to tell me.

(*He moves away.*)

LISA	Frank? I was only . . . Frank? Have I upset you? (*Pause.*) Making love . . . we've been making love, Frank . . .
FRANK	Fucking.
LISA	At first . . . not now . . .
FRANK	That's why you're here, ain't it?
LISA	Alright, if that's what you want . . . Yes.
FRANK	(*calm*) You fuck, I kill.
LISA	Frank, I don't want to fight . . .
FRANK	You fuck men, I kill 'em . . . easy . . . no fuckin' problem . . .
LISA	Look, I'm sorry if I've upset you, Frank, but I'm not taking that . . .
FRANK	You should write it all down, Lisa . . . every time we fuck you should write it down . . .
LISA	Right, I will, I'll keep a flamin' note pad by the bed.
FRANK	You do that . . .

LISA   I will.

FRANK   Good . . .

LISA   Fine . . .

FRANK   I'm gonna take a bath . . .

LISA   I'm sorry, Frank.

FRANK   I ain't never going back . . . never!

            (FRANK *exits. She shouts off to him, nervous*
            but trying to be jovial.)

LISA   I was thinkin', what with it nearly being
            Christmas an' that, I was thinkin' I'd like to
            go out and buy you a present . . . somethin'
            really nice like a watch or somethin'. Well, I
            shouldn't really tell you, should I? I mean, I
            don't want to spoil the surprise now, do I?
            Hey Frank, maybe I could buy a few
            decorations, brighten the place up a bit . . . I
            could even get us a Christmas tree . . . with
            fairy lights and an angel on top . . . oh, that'd
            be lovely, wouldn't it? I don't bother as a rule,
            let's face it, I practically live at the club . . .
            but a Christmas tree, well that'd make
            everything feel really special, wouldn't it?

            (FRANK *walks back on quietly. He looks at her*
            a moment.)

FRANK   I'm gonna tell Ron . . .

LISA   What?

FRANK   I'm gonna have to tell him about you . . .

LISA   (*laughs nervously*) What about me?

FRANK   Big house in the country, cows, sheep, even
            lambs, right?

LISA   Frank, what are you gonna tell him?

FRANK   Fields right? Big fields, fuckin' massive fields
                everywhere you look. All fields, all mine.

LISA   Everything I said, Frank, 'bout you giving
                yourself up . . . well, it's only because I care
                about you, you know that don't you? . . .
                Frank? You do know it, don't you?

FRANK   Yeah . . .

LISA   You do?

FRANK   Yeah . . . that's why . . .

LISA   What do you mean?

FRANK   That's why . . . why you're coming with me.

LISA   Where, Frank?

FRANK   Big house, fields, tractor, massive fields,
                everywhere you look, fields, my fields, mine
                and yours . . .

LISA   You want me to live in the country with you?

FRANK   You've got to, don't you see? That's why . . .
                why I came here, so you could find me. So we
                can live in the country with Ron . . .

LISA   With Ron? (*Laughs, trying to keep the
                atmosphere light.*) But Ron can't stand women
                'round him. He doesn't even like women,
                well, except for his mother. Frank . . . ? (*She
                laughs nervously.*) I can't live with you and
                Ron . . .

FRANK   You can . . . when we get married you can . . .

Scene Twelve

JOHN *on the sofa.* LISA *enters from the bedroom.*

LISA   John, I've got to go tonight. I've got to get out
                 of here . . .

JOHN   What's wrong?

LISA   Nothing, I'm just worried, I need to organise
                 things . . . I feel terrible, I can't let things go
                 on any longer. I've got to get out . . . I want to
                 go home.

JOHN   Tonight?

LISA   I've got to, John, I'm scared.

JOHN   'Cos you're pregnant?

LISA   Yes . . . no. Because of Frank, he won't have
                 it. He won't give himself up, and he means it.
                 He's not gonna go back, he believes
                 everything Ron tells him. He really believes
                 there's this big house in the country . . . John?
                 Did you hear what I said, he's really scaring
                 me . . .

JOHN   There is a house.

LISA   What?

JOHN   If Ron promised him a house in the country
                 then there is one. I spoke with Reg, and, well,
                 Reg says there is a house.

LISA   But . . .

JOHN   Look, Lisa, leave it out, eh?

LISA   Leave it out? John, he thinks I'm gonna be
                 living with him for God's sake . . .

                 (JOHN *laughs. He fixes them both a drink.*)

JOHN   Come on, relax. Have a drink?

LISA   Relax? John, how can I relax? He thinks we're
                gonna be getting married. Bleedin' 'ell, John,
                he thinks we're gonna be living with Ron.

JOHN   Lisa, listen darlin', let the crazy bastard think
                what he wants, eh? If it keeps him happy then
                it ain't gonna hurt now is it?

LISA   No . . . but I still wanna go home . . .

JOHN   If you leave, Lisa, you've got to come back.

LISA   I'm not stupid, John.

JOHN   You can't do a runner.

LISA   I know. (*Pause.*) Thanks, John.

JOHN   Don't thank me, Lisa. Just get yourself back
                here before Tarzan wakes.

                        Scene Thirteen

JOHN's *been drinking, and is dozing on the sofa.* FRANK *bursts
into the room from off stage.* JOHN *is edgy but tries to calm
him.*

FRANK   Where the fuck is she?

JOHN   Frank, calm down . . . I can explain.

FRANK   She's gone . . . she's fuckin' left me . . .

                (*He walks up to* JOHN. JOHN *is scared —* FRANK
                *grabs him, almost lifting him off the ground
                then forces his face down , hard, onto the
                phone.*)

JOHN   She's just nipped home, Frank, that's all . . .

FRANK   Get on the blower, get on the blower to Ron
               and tell him I want her back . . .

JOHN   Frank, she's coming back . . .

FRANK   This is you . . . this is your fault . . .

JOHN   Come on, mate, you're overreacting here . . .

FRANK   You let her fuckin' walk out . . .

JOHN   She'll be back, Frank, trust me . . .

               (FRANK *lets go of him.* JOHN *jumps up and
               backs away.*)

FRANK   Give me your gun . . .

JOHN   Frank, mate, come on . . .

FRANK   I said give me your bleedin' gun now.

JOHN   You know I can't do that, Frank . . .

FRANK   You let her just walk out on me.

JOHN   Frank, listen to me, you've got to calm down.

FRANK   I will . . . I am . . . look, I'm calm . . . just
               give me your bleedin' gun . . .

JOHN   She's gone for a couple of hours, Frank, no
               more, she's got things to sort out . . . she
               wanted to freshen up for you, Frank, you know
               what women are like, she wanted to change
               her clothes, look nice for you an' that . . .

FRANK   Gun . . . I want your gun, John . . .

JOHN   I can't give you it, Frank . . .

FRANK   I could break every bone in your body with
               just one hand, you do know that, don't you,
               John?

JOHN   Come on, Frank, we're mates, ain't we?

FRANK   I took the cat and the birch, I took six blokes kicking me when I was in a body harness. You ever seen one of them? You can't move . . . not even your head . . . I've taken everything they come at me with and they still couldn't break me . . . I picked up a piano once. I could have pelted it out the bleedin' window if I'd wanted . . . I ain't scared of no man . . . I'm like Tarzan . . . you ever seen Tarzan wrestle with a crocodile? I ain't scared of nothin' . . . 'cept dogs, big dogs. I once saw a bleedin' dog with metal fangs, John. I tell ya it was going fuckin' crazy . . . I hate bleedin' dogs, don't you?

JOHN   Yeah I do, Frank. Frank, why don't you get some rest, eh? And before you know it, Lisa'll be back . . . Frank?

FRANK   I escaped from Hull prison but ran the wrong way. I got trapped in the cemetery and tried to hide behind a giant angel, but it got me . . . I feel like that dog sometimes, I wanna hurt someone so fuckin' bad, John, I wanna rip 'em to shreds. They can't make me go back . . . no one can . . . I ain't never going back. Give me your gun, I wanna be ready. I wanna be ready when they come at me . . .

JOHN   No one's coming at you, Frank. Lisa'll be back soon.

FRANK   She's the best thing that's ever happened to me, John.

JOHN   I know, mate. Shall I make you some eggs?

FRANK   I had a budgie of me own once . . .

JOHN   Listen to me, Frank. It won't be long now.
                Lisa'll be back and soon you'll going to the
                country . . .

FRANK   I killed it.

JOHN   Ron's got it all arranged . . . remember,
                Frank?

FRANK   I killed it, John.

JOHN   You'll be well sorted by Christmas Day . . .

FRANK   If she doesn't come back I'm gonna have to
                hurt you, John.

JOHN   Frank, there's no need for all this, mate. You
                should trust me, you know, ain't I taken real
                good care of you up to now . . . eh?

FRANK   You're a good cook, John.

JOHN   Yeah? You like my cooking?

FRANK   You're a good cook, John. But you're a lousy
                fuckin' liar . . . if she's not back soon, you're
                dead.

                (FRANK *storms out, leaving* JOHN *alone and
                worried.*)

JOHN   Jesus, Lisa, where the hell are you? How did I
                get myself roped into this . . . come on . . .
                come on . . . stay calm, John . . . have a drink,
                John . . . I think I will . . . make mine a
                double . . . come on . . . come on . . .

                (FRANK *returns, calmer. He has a letter.*)

FRANK   I done this letter for Ron.

JOHN   What is it?

FRANK   What's it look like, it's a bleedin' letter.

JOHN   For Ron?

FRANK   Yeah, for Ron.

JOHN   (*light*) What's it say, Frank?

FRANK   It says I want some fuckin' answers, John. It
                says I ain't happy, I want Lisa back and I
                wanna get out . . . .

JOHN   But Frank, you know things ain't easy just
                now . . . Ron's havin' to lay low himself, mate
                . . . he's doing all he can.

FRANK   I want it taking to him now, John.

JOHN   Now?

FRANK   Yeah, now.

JOHN   But it's the middle of the night, Frank . . . I
                can't do it mate, I can't leave you here alone
                . . . what if someone calls, eh? What if the old
                bill show? Lisa's gonna be back soon Frank,
                and then I'll fix you both a nice big fry-up,
                eh? One of my specials, yeah?

FRANK   Get on the blower to Reg and tell him I've got
                a fuckin' letter for Ron . . .

JOHN   Come on, be reasonable, Frank . . .

FRANK   I want some fuckin' answers, John.

JOHN   Ain't I been giving you answers, Frank? Ain't
                I just told you you're gonna be in the country
                by Christmas, mate?

FRANK   You got a family, John?

JOHN   Yeah . . . I've got a mother, but she's up in
                Scotland.

FRANK   Would she care if she knew you were dead?

JOHN   She'd probably throw a party, mate, we ain't
            talked in years.

FRANK   John, I ain't asking again, if you don't take
            this letter to Ron, I'm going round the
            Vallance Road and I'm gonna see Ron's
            mother and I'm gonna have to frighten her,
            John . . . I'm gonna have to show them
            bastards that I want some answers . . .

JOHN   Come on, Frank, you know you don't mean
            that . . . do you? Frank? Look shall I fix you
            that fry-up now, eh? Shall I do you one of my
            specials?

FRANK   I've been banged up all my life, John . . . I
            wanna go home, and I want Lisa with me . . .

JOHN   I know you do, mate . . .

            (FRANK *grabs hold of his arm* — JOHN *cannot
            move.*)

FRANK   Give me your gun, John . . . I wanna go and
            shoot a copper.

JOHN   You can't do that, Frank . . .

FRANK   Get on the blower and tell Reg . . .

JOHN   Why don't we both calm down a bit first, eh?
            Relax, mate — 'ere, I'll fix you a drink . . .

FRANK   (*tightening his grip*) Tell them I'm gonna
            shoot a copper.

JOHN   Fuck, Frank! You know I can't do that . . .

FRANK   Tell Reg I've got a letter for Ron.

JOHN   Jesus Christ, mate, what are you trying to do
            to me? Look, I'm sorry Lisa's gone, Frank, I

tried to talk her into staying, I did. I told her
you'd go fuckin' mental . . . I told her you'd
be upset . . . but she insisted, you know, she
wanted to look nice for you, mate . . . she
wanted to change her dress an' that . . .
Frank, I think she's crazy about you, you
know . . . I think she's really trying to impress
you, mate.

(*Pause.* FRANK *lets go.*)

FRANK   I'd like to get her a present, John.

JOHN   (*relieved*) Yeah? A present? That's nice,
Frank, that's a great idea . . .

FRANK   I'd like to get her a budgie called Frank . . . a
yellow one.

(*He makes a budgie like sound and moves
closer to* JOHN.)

JOHN   That's great Frank, that's fan . . . tastic, mate.

(LISA *enters.*)

FRANK   You left me.

JOHN   Right, well, I'll see to that fry-up shall I?

(JOHN *exits quckly.*)

LISA   No, Frank, I just went home for a while . . .

FRANK   (*matter of fact*) I wanna go home. I wanna see
my mother.

LISA   You will, Frank . . . soon you will.

Scene Fourteen

JOHN *is sitting drinking in the dark. It is a short while after
the previous scene.* JOHN *is pissed off with* LISA. *She is aware*

of this and is trying to lighten things. JOHN *swigs back a large one.* LISA *walks on and lights a cigarette in the dark. Lights snap up.*

LISA   You know what they say about drinking alone . . .

JOHN   Yeah, I do — and it's bollocks . . .

LISA   *(taking the drink from him)* Is it?

                  (She takes a sip, hands it back.)

JOHN   Don't you think you better get back in there, Lisa, make up for lost time?

LISA   You look tired, John . . .

JOHN   You look old . . .

LISA   Thanks . . .

JOHN   Don't mention it . . .

LISA   What's in this for you, John?

JOHN   Lisa . . . you're not being paid to open your mouth . . . know what I mean?

LISA   What's wrong, John . . . make you nervous, do I?

JOHN   Just stick to what you do best, eh?

LISA   How would you know what I do best?

JOHN   Well, I don't see you singing yourself rich.

LISA   And what about you?

JOHN   What about me?

LISA   *(pouring herself a drink)* What do you do best?

JOHN	I keep my mind on the job.
LISA	I bet you do . . .
JOHN	You'd do well to do the same . . .

(FRANK *enters. He's in a mood.*)

FRANK	What you doin'?
LISA	I was just coming . . .
FRANK	What's that?
LISA	What do you mean?
FRANK	That!
LISA	It's a drink.
FRANK	I can see it's a drink, Lisa . . .
JOHN	It's only a drink, Frank . . .
FRANK	I'm not asking you . . . why are you drinking?
LISA	Jesus, Frank, I fancied a drink . . .
FRANK	With him?
LISA	I was just coming back to bed.
FRANK	What's that smell?
LISA	What?
FRANK	You. You smell different . . .
LISA	I . . . it's my perfume, Frank . . . it's French . . . I thought you might like it . . . Frank, I wore it for you . . .

FRANK	I can smell you all the time . . . I can't breathe . . . you're suffocating me . . .
JOHN	Go and wash it off.
LISA	What? Shall I, Frank? Shall I wash it off? Frank? . . .
FRANK	Why do you wear it?
JOHN	Frank, she only wanted to smell nice for you, mate . . .
FRANK	I know why . . . I know why you wear it. It's 'cos of me . . . 'cos you think I stink.
LISA	I don't . . . I don't understand, Frank . . . why would I think that, you're always washing . . .
FRANK	I can smell meself . . . I'm turning bad . . . I smell like the river, the bit that's blocked from the rest, the bit that's never gonna reach the sea . . . the bit that's full of shit . . .
LISA	I like the way you smell.
FRANK	The bit full of dead bodies.
JOHN	I'll . . . I'll go and run you a bath, shall I mate?
FRANK	What do you want from me?
LISA	I want . . . you. No gun to me head, no axe under the bed . . . just you . . . I'm going to bed.

(LISA *exits*.)

JOHN	It was only one drink, Frank . . .
FRANK	Send out for some flowers, John.
JOHN	She's . . . she's crazy about you, Frank.

FRANK   Flowers, John . . . roses . . . yellow roses.

JOHN   It's the middle of the night, Frank.

FRANK   No, red . . . red roses. Good ones, no cheap
                 crap . . . red ones . . . the best, John. I want
                 Lisa to have the best.

JOHN   I know you do, Frank . . . Frank — listen to
                 me, mate, I cannot get roses at this time of
                 night . . . it's impossible, Frank, I would if I
                 could, mate, but it's just, it's just not possible,
                 mate. Frank? Frank, how about I fix you both
                 some eggs, eh, Frank? I'll even cut the bread
                 up real nice an' that. Put it round the egg like
                 the sun . . . Frank?

FRANK   Sharks, John . . .

JOHN   Not too soft, not too hard . . . just how you
                 like 'em, eh, Frank?

FRANK   Sharks, John, they're only little, see, but it's
                 their teeth, John. They're all sharp teeth, see,
                 sharp as razors, they are . . .

JOHN   Yeah . . . yeah, I suppose they are, Frank.

FRANK   And sharks right, they can smell blood from
                 fuckin' miles away.

JOHN   Yeah, that right? Blood, eh? Fuck . . .

FRANK   But dolphins, they just know, see, they know
                 everything, John.

JOHN   Dolphins, right . . . that's nice, Frank . . .
                 dolphins. I . . . I like dolphins . . .

FRANK   Yeah? You do? Good, good, 'cos dolphins
                 know everything, they just know, see . . . 'cos
                 they sleep with one eye open, John . . . one
                 eye sleep, the other one awake. Watching, see,

watching and waiting . . . they don't have to
smell the blood, they just hear the crying . . .
from fuckin' miles away . . . one eye asleep,
the other one awake. Just listening. Waiting
. . . knowing they're next. First thing in the
morning I want red roses, John . . . I want this
room filled with them.

Scene Fifteen

LISA *and* FRANK *are fooling around like kids, blowing up red*
balloons which now fill the room. JOHN *sits watching them.*

FRANK   Come on, John, blow some up. You know
               you're full of hot air, mate.

               (LISA *and* FRANK *laugh.*)

LISA   Oh I can't remember the last time I laughed so
               much. John, ain't it been a laugh?

JOHN   (*dry*) Oh yeah, Lisa, it's been a bleedin'
               scream . . .

LISA   (*quietly*) You're drinking too much . . .

JOHN   You talk too much.

FRANK   'Ere, we could fill the whole bleedin' room
               with 'em . . . 'ere John, I think we need some
               more, mate.

JOHN   They'll have to do, mate . . .

LISA   Oh go on, John, Frank's right, let's go mad,
               eh?

JOHN   Look around, Lisa, we're there already . . .

LISA   It's only a bit of fun . . . come on, John.
               Lighten up . . . let's have some fun, eh?

JOHN   (*holding his drink up*) This is all the fun I
                need, alright?

LISA   Please yourself . . . (*She moves closer to*
                FRANK.) Mmmm — can you smell that turkey,
                Frank?

FRANK   Yeah . . . I ain't never 'ad Christmas dinner
                with a girlfriend.

JOHN   Don't suppose you have . . .

LISA   (*moves to* JOHN) Come on, John, cheer up.
                Let's make it really special for him, yeah?

JOHN   I think that's your job . . . don't you?

FRANK   Is it gonna be ready soon?

LISA   Yes . . . how long's it been in, John?

JOHN   You saw to it, Lisa . . .

FRANK   'Ere, John, we don't want to cremate the
                bastard!

LISA   I'll check on it . . .

                (LISA *exits.*)

JOHN   Yeah, you do that.

FRANK   'Ere, John, that turkey's a big fucker, ain't it?

JOHN   Yeah, it is, Frank . . .

FRANK   I reckon Reg got the biggest in the place,
                don't you?

JOHN   Yeah, I suppose he did. Let's face it, if the
                twins want something, they get it, knowing
                them, it'll 'ave been fattened up all year
                round . . .

FRANK   I ain't never seen a turkey like it, John. It's
                fucking massive, and I mean it's a full one,
                ain't it? Jesus, the only thing missing is its
                bleedin' head. I bet it's gonna taste good,
                don't you, John?

JOHN   Let's hope so, Frank . . .

FRANK   I bet Lisa's a good cook, don't you?

JOHN   Well, we'll soon find out . . .

FRANK   'Ere, John — when me and Lisa's married you
                can come and visit us in the country and she'll
                cook turkey and we can have a few drinks an'
                that . . .

JOHN   Yeah . . . yeah, I'd like that . . .

FRANK   I'm gonna keep wild ponies you know, like the
                ones on Dartmoor. Can you imagine it, John?

JOHN   What, mate?

FRANK   Being out there, in the country, an' that. I
                won't 'ave to stay indoors no more. I'll never
                have to be locked in at night, or be told when
                to eat and sleep. 'Ere, John, I'll never have to
                shit in no friggin' tin bucket neither!

JOHN   (*looking at him, smiling*) No, don't suppose
                you will, mate.

FRANK   I'm gonna 'ave me own keys an' everything.

JOHN   Keys?

FRANK   Yeah, to a door, my door. Fuckin' 'ell, John,
                keys, right, keys to me own front door.
                Everyone 'as keys, don't they, John?

JOHN   Yeah . . . suppose they do, mate.

FRANK   I ain't never 'ad no keys. I ain't never 'ad me
                own door, see, only one someone else locks.
                I've seen them bastards with their fuckin'
                massive bunches of keys. I've seen 'em
                fuckin' swinging 'em in my face, John,
                locking the cell door, turning the light off and
                laughing at me, I'm gonna show 'em all, ain't
                I, John? I'm gonna show all them bastards
                that I've got the fuckin' keys now . . .

LISA   (*bursting in, excitedly*) Right, gents, dinner is
                almost ready, and though I say so myself it's
                done to perrr-fection.

FRANK   Did you hear that, John? Ain't she fantastic,
                ain't she beautiful, John?

JOHN   Yeah, she's beautiful, mate.

LISA   Frank, why don't you help me in the kitchen?

                (FRANK *and* LISA *exit to the kitchen. The phone
                rings.* JOHN *picks it up, talks quickly in a
                whisper.*)

JOHN   Yeah? Yeah, yeah, right. No, no problem —
                sweet, no that's great . . .

                (FRANK *and* LISA *enter.*)

                (*attempting to be light tone*) Yeah, I'll tell
                him, yeah. (*To* FRANK.) He wants to know if
                you liked the bird?

FRANK   (*looks at* LISA) Yeah, I do, I bleedin' love 'er,
                John . . .

JOHN   I think they meant the turkey, Frank.

LISA   Tell 'em it's smashing . . .

JOHN   Yeah, yeah . . . the bird's a beauty, thanks . . .

                (FRANK *goes back to the kitchen.*)

Yeah, I'll do that, no, no problem . . . no. It'll be sweet . . . yeah, easy . . . I'll see to it. Right . . .

(*He puts the phone down.*)

LISA   Everything OK, John?

JOHN   I've never liked that word, Lisa, never trusted it. In fact I've always thought it was a stupid fuckin' word, totally over-used. Know what I mean?

LISA   What word?

JOHN   (*edgy*) 'OK' . . . I mean what the fuck does 'OK' mean? Eh? Can you tell me that? Can you tell me what 'OK' fuckin' means?

LISA   Well, you know what —

JOHN   Do I?

LISA   What's wrong? Don't spoil things, John . . .

(FRANK *has silently re-entered. Now he suddenly bursts a balloon.*)

LISA   Jesus, Frank . . .

FRANK   'Ere, shall I burst 'em all?

LISA   Right, well, I'll get that bottle of wine, shall I?

JOHN   I'll get it . . .

LISA   No! No, I'm perfectly capable of opening a bottle of wine, thank you . . . ooooh . . . (*She holds her stomach.*)

JOHN   What is it?

LISA   Nothing . . . just a stitch, must be all that balloon blowing . . .

JOHN   I'll see to the wine . . .

(FRANK *bursts another balloon.*)

LISA   (*snaps, holding her stomach*) Frank, please! Don't burst any more, there'll be none left . . . (*She sits down amongst the balloons.*) Don't burst them . . . they're so pretty. (*She holds one up to the light.*) They're almost perfect, look . . . so bright and colourful and —

(FRANK *bursts it out of her hands.*)

LISA   Perfect . . .

Scene Sixteen

FRANK *and* LISA *dance to Frank Sinatra's "Something Stupid".*
JOHN *sets up the Christmas tree. As the song fades,* FRANK
exits.

LISA   Doesn't it look lovely, John? There's something so magical about a Christmas tree . . . you know, all lit up. He's sleeping . . . like a baby. (*Pause.*) It was a smashing turkey . . .

(*Still no reaction from* JOHN.)

LISA   (*trying to be light*) I've never seen a man eat so much . . . (*Laughs.*) Still, he enjoyed himself . . .

JOHN   Well, it'll be over soon . . .

LISA   Yeah, true.

JOHN   Tonight.

LISA   Tonight?

JOHN   They're comin' for him . . .

LISA   Who?

JOHN   Few of the boys . . . they're sending a van.

LISA   To take him to the country?

JOHN   Yeah, yeah . . . do you want a drink?

LISA   No . . . don't you think you've had enough?

JOHN   (*short*) I'm still standing.

                (*He pours himself a drink.*)

LISA   John. Is it to take him to the country?

JOHN   Yeah . . .

LISA   You sure?

JOHN   (*short*) Yes! It's to take him to the country . . .

                (*Pause.*)

LISA   Yeah, good. When?

JOHN   Early hours, when it's quiet . . .

LISA   Christmas Day . . . that'll be Christmas Day,
                John.

JOHN   Exactly . . . thank you, Father bleedin'
                Christmas . . .

                (*Downs his drink in one and pours another.
                Pause.*)

LISA   So when are you gonna tell him?

JOHN	I'm not. Well, not until I have to. That's what the twins want me to do, so that's what I do, right?
LISA	(*watching him closely*) Right . . . yeah . . .
JOHN	Yeah, that's what I do . . . and I tell him about you.
LISA	Me?
JOHN	About you now going . . . they say to let him think you're gonna be joining him later . . .
LISA	Oh, right . . . yeah, good. But I'm not, am I John?

(*Pause. She waits for a reaction.*)

I don't have to, do I?

JOHN	Do you want to?
LISA	(*hesitant*) No . . . you know I don't.
JOHN	(*sarcastic*) Are you sure, Lisa? You mean to say you don't wanna see this big lovely country house of his?
LISA	No . . . you know I don't . . . (*She studies him closely.*) Everything's going to be alright, isn't it, John?
JOHN	Yeah . . . sweet . . . no problem.
LISA	Good . . . and the rest of the money?

(JOHN *does not react.*)

My two hundred . . . John? You did say . . .

JOHN	We've gotta clean this place up, when he's gone. Wet cloth, dry cloth, know what I mean? As if he was never here . . .

LISA   Oh, yeah, I see . . . and my money?

JOHN   So he's sleepin', yeah?

LISA   Yeah . . . the money, John? What about my
            money?

JOHN   You've got to go to a party . . .

LISA   A party?

JOHN   Yeah, a Christmas party. Reg'll be there.
            He'll, er, probably sort you out . . .

LISA   Probably? John? I will get what I'm owed,
            won't I?

JOHN   Lisa, we don't ask questions, we just do what
            they say, alright?

            (*Silence. Both are deep in thought.*)

LISA   God, John. I can't believe it, I mean, not
            being here, no more Frank. (*Laughs fondly.*)
            Tarzan, eh?

JOHN   Yeah. Champion Amongst Men . . .

LISA   He'll be alright though, won't he? I mean,
            they'll look after him?

JOHN   Yeah, they'll look after him . . .

LISA   I can see him, you know, looking after all his
            animals. He's funny that way, isn't he? You
            know, gentle. I mean, with animals. Maybe
            it's because his dad worked in a
            slaughterhouse.

JOHN   Look, why don't you go back to bed?

LISA   In a bit. Let him sleep. (*Pause.*) Do you know
            what he told me, John? He said that when you

kill a cow it doesn't die straight off, it sort of
twitches. And then you see it, it does this last
big jump . . . and that's it . . . it's gone.

JOHN   Gone?

LISA   Yeah. Dead. It's jumped to cow heaven, ain't
              that sad, John. It's so sad, yet, yet sort of
              lovely as well.

JOHN   (*light, half-laugh*) I think you're turning soft,
              girl . . .

LISA   (*smiles*) Yeah . . . think I must be.

JOHN   Look, they'll be coming about two, so I think
              you should get back in there and . . . you
              know, keep him company an' that.

LISA   Yeah, maybe you're right.

JOHN   I'll get his things ready. Poor bastard, he ain't
              got much, just his radio, change of shirt . . .

LISA   (*looking at the tree*) I'm glad we got a tree,
              made it special. (*Beat.*) So did they tell you
              where this house in the country was? (*Silence.
              LISA studies him.*) No . . . no, of course not.

              (*She begins to leave, stops. Looks around at
              the balloons.*)

LISA   I should have let him burst all his balloons . . .

              Scene Seventeen

LISA *picked out in a spotlight.*

LISA   I lay in bed under him and I feel myself sort of
              twitching, or is it flinching . . . or am I just
              shaking? Whilst he pounds away on top of me
              . . . pushing me down into a dark place, his
              whole body smothering me . . . and I close my

eyes and I try to hold myself together and I try
to fly up and out the boarded-up window, over
the rooftops and down the river, and
everything is grey and cold and I just think, if
I could just get a bit higher . . . past the
clouds and into the sun, maybe I might find
something better, maybe I might even find
heaven. But then I hear him crying . . . or is it
me? Maybe it's both of us . . . and then I feel
him twitching . . . until he jumps and he
jumps me back to hell. Flat on me back, a ton
of weight on top of me . . . and a dirty river
inside me. But I like its smell, it's a smell I
know. It's a smell I have to love . . . don't I?

Scene Eighteen

LISA *holds up a bed sheet to reveal a large patch of blood.
Just then* JOHN *walks in.* JOHN *notices the blood.*

LISA   I've stripped the bed.

JOHN   Frank's getting ready . . . they'll be coming
                for him soon.

LISA   Right . . . good.

JOHN   You alright?

LISA   Yeah, yeah. Look, give me a few minutes . . .

JOHN   Oh . . . yeah . . . right.

                (*She rolls the sheet into a bundle and holds it
                like a baby. Hold the moment as the lights
                fade.*)

Scene Nineteen

JOHN *puts the telephone down.*

LISA   Was that them?

JOHN	Yeah . . .
LISA	Is he still in the bathroom?
JOHN	Yeah . . . you alright?
LISA	I will be.
JOHN	Did he . . . you know, see anything?
LISA	No . . .
JOHN	You sure you're alright?
LISA	Yes, I'm fine, look, let's just see to Frank . . .
JOHN	Frank's happy, he's excited, yeah. He's well sorted . . .
LISA	And he knows I'm not going?
JOHN	Yeah, yeah.
LISA	And he was alright about it?
JOHN	No he went crazy and threw me out the bleedin' window. 'Course he was alright. Lisa, the man's happy just to be going.
LISA	So you told him I'd be joining him later?
JOHN	Yeah, he thinks you're going home to pack.
LISA	Good . . . I've got him a Christmas card . . .
JOHN	Yeah? Well I think he's done you one . . .
LISA	Has he?
JOHN	Yeah, he's done loads, even the Governor of Dartmoor's got one, he only wanted me to post it . . . I tell you, now the bloke thinks he's going on his bleedin' holidays . . .

(*Pause.*)

LISA   But they're taking him to the house, right?

JOHN   Right. Jesus, what does he do in there?

LISA   And they'll be here soon, won't they?

JOHN   I bleedin' hope so, girl . . .

LISA   I wonder if it's still snowing? I bet it's lovely
                in the country, you know, with all those hills
                covered with snow . . . I've never stood on a
                hill covered in snow . . . I don't think I've
                ever stood on a hill . . . isn't that daft . . .
                fancy never havin' stood on a hill . . .

JOHN   Jesus, Frank . . . I better go and get him.

                (JOHN *exits.* LISA *has a moment alone.* FRANK
                enters, wearing a jacket and hat.)

LISA   Frank . . . you look nice . . .

FRANK   John told me . . . you know, what Ron said . . .
                'bout you coming to the country later . . . He
                reckons it's safer an' that . . . I told him I
                think that's a good idea, Lisa, 'cos I think
                there might still be loads of coppers an' that
                . . . you know, out there still looking for me
                an' that . . . I don't want you getting into any
                bother, Lisa.

LISA   No, I understand . . .

FRANK   You don't mind, do you? Lisa?

LISA   No . . . no I don't mind . . . Frank?

FRANK   I've got you a card . . .

LISA   I've got you one as well . . . Frank?

FRANK   It's here . . . this is for you, Lisa . . . it's a
        Christmas card . . .

LISA   Oh . . . Frank? Frank, I want to . . .

        (*The doorbell rings.* JOHN *crosses the stage
        and exits in a hurry.*)

JOHN   That'll be them, Frank . . . you got
        everything? Yeah . . . yeah . . . good, great.
        Don't forget your radio . . . right. I'll . . . I'll
        see to the door . . .

FRANK   It's them . . . they're here now . . . I'm going
        now, Lisa . . .

LISA   Frank, I wanted to . . . (*She kisses him.*) . . .
        kiss you goodbye . . .

FRANK   I remembered things . . . things I wanted to
        tell you . . . things I thought I'd forgot . . .

JOHN   Frank, they're waiting . . .

FRANK   'Bout other animals and that . . .

LISA   They'll keep, Frank . . . I'll see you soon . . .

JOHN   Frank . . .

FRANK   Like elephants, Lisa, did you know they can't
        even jump, and, and if you leave a goldfish in
        the dark, right, it turns white? (*Laughs.*)
        Fuckin' white, John . . .

JOHN   Yeah? White? Fuck, that's amazing, Frank —
        Frank, they're ready . . .

FRANK   And snails, right. Snails can crawl along the
        edge of a razor blade and not even hurt
        themselves . . .

JOHN   Frank, the boys are waiting . . .

LISA   Look after yourself, Frank . . .

FRANK   No . . . wait, this is the best, wait, the glow
                from a firefly, right?

JOHN   Save it for later, eh Frank?

LISA   No! No, let him . . . tell me, Frank. What is
                it? The glow from the firefly . . .

JOHN   Jesus, Lisa . . .

FRANK   It's bright enough to shine through the belly
                of a frog, you know, the frog that's eaten it,
                ain't that clever? Ain't that beautiful?

JOHN   Yeah . . . it's beautiful, Frank . . . so can we
                go now?

FRANK   I wanted to get you a present, Lisa. It's my
                comb . . .

LISA   Oh, thank you, Frank. It's lovely.

FRANK   It's for your hair an' that . . .

JOHN   Frank, they're waiting, mate.

                (FRANK *goes to leave, then turns back.*)

FRANK   Don't forget to bring your chocolates, Lisa . . .

                (LISA *looks at them.*)

FRANK   You can open them on Christmas Day . . .

LISA   No . . . I won't forget . . .

                (*He exits.*)

LISA   But it's Christmas Day now, darlin' . . .

Scene Twenty

JOHN *is frantically bursting the red balloons.* LISA *dashes on.*

LISA   John, what was that? I heard it from the bedroom, it sounded like gunshots . . .

JOHN   It was me bursting these bleeding things . . .

LISA   Oh God, John . . . is he going to be alright?

JOHN   He's gone now, don't worry . . .

LISA   Christ, John, I'm scared . . .

JOHN   Lisa look, you'd better get ready . . .

LISA   I don't want to go to their party, John, I want to go home . . .

JOHN   Just get ready, eh?

LISA   I'm scared, I'm scared for Frank. Jesus, John, I heard gunshots, I know I did . . .

JOHN   Lisa, listen to me, you've got to calm down — there were no gunshots, alright? None. It was just me bursting balloons, you've got to watch what you say, alright?

LISA   We should have let Frank burst them . . . he wanted to.

JOHN   (*snaps*) Frank's gone . . . alright? If I was you, Lisa, I'd forget all about Frank. Just go and get ready and a car'll be here for you soon . . .

LISA   A car?

JOHN   What was all that shit about a firefly, eh?

LISA   A car, John? Whose car? Who's picking me up?

JOHN   Its glow is bright enough to be seen in the
              belly of a frog, what the fuck does that mean,
              eh?

LISA   John, I don't want to go in any car . . .

JOHN   'Cos if it's been eaten it's got to be fuckin'
              dead, ain't it?

LISA   John, please. Not on my own . . .

JOHN   What do you think, Lisa?

LISA   What?

JOHN   The little firefly, is it dead, or just in hiding?

LISA   I don't know . . . John, if I've got to go to this
              party will you come with me?

JOHN   Jesus, look . . .

              (*He picks up* FRANK'S *mask.*)

LISA   If I've got to go to this party will you come
              with me, John?

JOHN   He made it himself . . .

LISA   John, will you? Will you come in the car with
              me? I'm scared, John, I don't want to go in
              any car on my own . . . (*She holds her
              stomach.*)

JOHN   Look, you'll be OK . . . Don't worry, Lisa . . .

LISA   Oh God, John. (*She doubles up in pain.*)
              Please, please say you'll come with me . . .

JOHN   Are you alright?

LISA   I'm scared . . .

JOHN   Fuck, what can I do?

LISA	I don't want to go in the car . . .
JOHN	But they'll be here soon, fuck, Lisa, you have to, you know. You've got go to Reg's party, show him everything's alright . . .
LISA	I will go. I will go — but not in a car — not on my own. (*Pause.*) Will you, John? Will you come with me?
JOHN	Yes, no — fuck, I don't know . . .

(*He puts the mask in the pillowcase he has been using to dispose of* FRANK'S *things. He puts the chocolates into the pillowcase. The phone rings.*)

JOHN   That's them. They're on their way.

(*He goes to put* FRANK'S *Christmas card into the pillowcase.*)

LISA   No, John, read it. Read what it says.

JOHN   To Lisa. The only girl I ever loved. Happy Christmas, love Frank.

LISA   When you kill a cow it doesn't die straight off, it sort of twitches, and then you see it, it does this last big jump and that's it, it's gone.

(*The lights fade.*)